AROMATHERAPY

AROMATHERAPY

CATHY COOPER

SELECT EDITIONS

ACKNOWLEDGEMENT

For practical advice and expertise,
grateful thanks go to Allyson Hurst,
the knowledgeable owner of The Aroma Shop,
Carlisle Indoor Market.

CONSULTANT

Joanna Drew

This edition first published in 1995 by
Promotional Reprint Company Ltd,
Deacon House,
65 Old Church Street,
London SW3 5BS
for Selecta Book Ltd, Devizes, Wiltshire, UK

ISBN 1 85648 280 4

Printed and bound in China

PUBLISHER'S NOTE

Neither the publisher nor the author takes any responsibility for the implementation of any ideas, recommendations or techniques expressed and described in this book. Any use to which the ideas, recommendations and techniques are put is at the reader's sole discretion and risk.

CONTENTS

*You may break, you may shatter the vase,
if you will,*

*But the scent of the roses will hang
around it still.*

THOMAS MOORE
(1779-1852)

INTRODUCTION

It is possible to make an essential oil out of any plant, from violet through cauliflower and cactus to giant redwood, but there are only about 160 essential oils which are applied in aromatherapy.

These 160 oils create a complex and fascinating science. Each one of them has several uses, and can be blended with other oils to create yet other effects. However, many oils are similar in practical use and so duplicate each other. And some of them, if you consult a traditional aromatherapy manual, are credited with so many marvellous and beneficial properties that you wonder why on earth anybody needs the rest of the 159 oils.

Obviously you don't need to know every little thing about even half of them. It cannot matter to readers who just want to be able to benefit from aromatherapy, that essential oil of snakeroot is a febrifuge, that is to say that it has a cooling effect, for instance in a fever. Firstly, oils such as snakeroot are fairly obscure and difficult to obtain in your local high street. In the second place, aromatherapy does not pretend to take the place of medical science in such cases.

It may be of interest to apprentice aromatherapists to learn that hyacinth oil – a sedative and a hypnotic – can be used to try and improve the creative side of the brain. Most people, however, would rather improve their aching backs and/or their love life, or simply create a pleasant living environment, and for this reason this guide will concentrate on these practical areas.

So what do you need to know about aromatherapy? This book will guide you to the most important points, leaving aside the million-and-one superfluous, science-blinding details.

You need to know:

•How to use essential oils.

There are really just four ways and only one of those, massage, requires any special techniques.

•Which oils are the most useful.

In this book there is a Top Ten which will cover pretty well most people's basic needs, and a secondary group of suggested oils which you can follow up to expand on this beginner's kit, if you wish. The rest need not concern anyone but the most expert expert.

•How aromatherapy can help with the things that matter most.

By far the most widespread and frequent uses of aromatherapy are:

- As a relaxant, relieving mental stress and physical tensions
- As a pick-up when the going gets tough
- Easing everyday aches and pains
- Helping with skin care

- Helping with sleeping
- Adding spice to romance

Aromatherapy can help in many varied situations; it can be adapted to suit different lifestyles and enhance the quality of daily existence.

Most people care about their looks; a healthy appearance is a valuable boost to your self-esteem and social image, and aromatherapy can help here too.

It's not absolutely necessary but you might be interested to read what an essential oil actually is, how it is made, and how modern aromatherapy developed from ancient times.

Plant essences are used in various ways and not only for their aromatic powers. Herbal medicine was once far more widespread than it is now, and in those times herbal remedies were not 'alternative'; they were the only effective form of medicine that anybody knew about.

Jesse Boot, first Lord Trent and founder of Boots the Chemist, began as a young man in the 1870s by making herbal remedies, following his father's recipes. After well over 100 years of neglect, the wheel has come full circle and now many of the big drug and toiletry companies are offering herbal and aromatherapy products.

Plus, finally, a warning note. You need to be careful with substances as concentrated as essential oils.

Although most of the freely available oils are harmless in all usual circumstances, some do need to be treated with caution and this book will point that out wherever necessary.

Your Sunburst Handguide to Aromatherapy will give you enough basic information to start you using essential oils with confidence and, like any good introductory course, it will show you just a little of the world beyond.

THE BASICS

A dozen red roses can set off a romantic chain of events, and a few drops of the oil can have the same potential. In fact, oil of rose is a versatile essence with all sorts of uses in physical and mental therapy, but while many other oils have many similar uses, only a few have such a close association with romance.

Poets have sung for thousands of years about the magic of the rose. In aromatherapy, most beginners and home practitioners will have to forgo the pleasure of using this oil because of the cost. If you were thinking of buying essential oil of rose as a birthday present for an aromatic friend, pause and consider. By weight, gold is cheaper.

First practical point: what is aromatherapy going to cost you? Luckily for those without rich admirers, most of the useful oils are affordable. Three or four people could easily spend more on a night at a restaurant than the price of setting yourself up with the Top Ten oils, and you could get two complete sets of these for the price of one phial of rose oil. So, aromatherapy need not be expensive.

But just what is it that you are buying? For a start, a so-called essential oil is really more like a spirit-essence than an oil. Oils such as olive or sunflower are greasy, turgid substances which do not readily evaporate into the air. Essential oils, these essences in their little dark glass bottles, are thin, watery liquids which evaporate before your very eyes.

The technical term is **volatile,** and the chemical names of the myriad constituents of these volatile spirits usually end in '-of', '-ate' or '-ene', as in other volatile fluids such as alcohol, acetate and trinitrotoluene, or TNT. Leave the top off your phial and forget about it, and next time you look the phial will be empty.

As essential oils evaporate they carry and develop their scent, but the scent is often unrecognisably strong if sniffed neat. Some essential oils can smell less like a garden of flowers than like something you would wave under the nose of a boxer who had just been knocked out.

You now know how to recognise an essential oil. It is not oily, it may smell so strong it makes your eyes water, and if you put a drop on a tissue the wet mark will disappear very quickly.

The other types of oils you will come across are fragrant oils and carrier oils. Fragrant oils smell pleasant, are oily and do not evaporate as fast as essential oils. They are especially made for atmospheric uses such as pot pourri and aroma rings. They do not have the beneficial qualities of essential oils, just the same smell, and are only for fun.

Carrier oils are the medium by which a tiny bit of essence can be made to go a long way – for example in massage. Any kind of cold-pressed, additive-free vegetable oil could be used, but you might find olive or groundnut a bit overpowering and so, rather than raiding the kitchen cupboard, you are probably safer and better off buying professional carrier oils, also called fixed oils. You only use a very small quantity anyway, you know they are pure, and they even have limited beneficial effects in themselves which can help the essential oils to work.

METHODS

Using essential oils with water

If the king of aromatherapy methods is massage, the queen has to be the aromatic bath. A few drops of well-chosen essential oils, swirled into a not-too-hot bath (evaporation, remember), can relax you when you're all wound up, or can revive you when you thought you wanted to crawl away and hide.

Certain oils in the bath can ease pain, invigorate and unknot your tired and tense muscles, and give your skin a treat. Some oils can even act positively against infections.

If you ever have the chance, try your oils in a jacuzzi – it is fun, although rather extravagant – and next time you go to a sauna take a little phial of oil with you. A few drops added to that pan of water and then splashed on the hot stones can add a whole new dimension to a sauna.

You could try oil of the white birch, *Betula alba*. It is with the twigs of this tree that Scandinavians reputedly beat each other during their sauna rituals. White birch is very good for the skin and the circulation, and the aroma reminds you of after-shave of the 'leather' type, which is no coincidence because they use birch tar oil to make such products.

Another versatile water method is steam inhalation. Put a tea-towel over your head, close your eyes and breathe in the vapours from about

23 cm/9 inches above a steaming bowl. This can be good for all sorts of nasal and chest problems, headaches and colds, and can be effective as a form of facial, although avoid this method if you have sensitive skin, since it can produce broken or 'thread' veins. It is also a convenient way of using the powers of essential oils to relieve anxiety or give yourself a quick lift when you're feeling down.

Using essential oils with applicators

Compresses are the main way of applying oils directly to the body. Half fill a pudding basin with water – hot if you are treating muscular aches and stiffness in the joints, cold if the problem is a headache or a strained or pulled muscle. Add up to five drops of the oil, soak a clean piece of cotton cloth in the solution, gently squeeze out the surplus and hold to the affected part for as long as you feel it is doing good. Renew as necessary.

Oils can also be inhaled neat, and it is best to do this with some sort of portable 'sniffer', which need be nothing more complex than a small pill bottle with cotton wool inside with a few drops of oil added. This can be carried wherever you go.

Using essential oils with vapourisers

You could be really basic about this and simply fill a saucer with water, stand it on the radiator, then sprinkle in a few drops of oil. Alternatively, you could do it in style with a burner or a vapouriser. Burners come in all shapes and materials, the basic idea being to use a night-light candle to generate just enough heat to send the molecules of essential oil out into the atmosphere of the room. As long as you can wash all traces of oil off the burner before you next use it, it doesn't really matter which sort of burner you have.

Another very simple but luxurious method is the light-bulb ring. These little circular troughs fit over the bulb in the table-lamp or bedside-lamp and do the same job as the burners. You can use fragrant rather than essential oils in these atmospheric ways. You only get the aroma, not the therapy, but this may not matter in most cases. In serious applications you probably would not use the light and mild atmospheric methods anyway.

These methods are best suited to creating moods, freshening the air and making the environment more attractive to friends and lovers, or less attractive to insects. The aroma alone is usually sufficient in these cases. Fragrant or essential oils can be used to revive pot pourri, and some can be dabbed neat onto the skin as perfumes, for instance geranium, patchouli and sandalwood.

Using essential oils with massage

Aromatherapy without massage is like a holiday without sunshine – good, but nothing like as good as it should be. Massage improves the effects of the oils so that the combined result is the greater. One and one makes three when you add essential oil to massage. However, this is also the only method in aromatherapy that requires skill and the knowledge of correct technique. It is important to visit only a qualified masseur, and if your interest progresses, perhaps you could enrol yourself on a course to learn the essential skills.

Some simple rules of common sense must be applied:

- **Don't** massage infected or broken skin.
- **Don't** massage someone who is not in a fit state to be massaged, such as under the influence of drink or drugs. Check with a general practitioner if in doubt about the interaction of any prescribed medicine with the aromatherapy oils.
- **Don't** massage if you are not in a fit state.

Make sure the room and the general atmosphere are suitable. This is a relaxing, indulgent experience; it will work better in the sitting room with soft lights and sweet music rather than on the kitchen table with glaring fluorescent tubes and disco beat. Caring aroma-masseurs and masseusses might draw the curtains and use candlelight, accompanied by appropriate mood music.

Just use a little oil. Adding a drop more to the hands is much easier than trying to wipe away a highly aromatic excess oozing all over the place. A teaspoonful of carrier oil with two or three drops of essential oil should be more than enough to do a complete back massage. Increasing the proportion of essential oil will not necessarily increase the effect, and indeed it may act to the detriment of the therapeutic treatment.

There are scores of carrier or fixed oils. You can get avocado or fractionated coconut if you want, but the cheapest and most widely used general purpose carriers are grapeseed and sweet almond. Similar but with different qualities are wheatgerm and jojoba, which you can add to your blend (essentials only, or essentials plus carrier) at a proportion of about 10 per cent to enrich it. Wheatgerm is especially good for facials, and it is a preservative which helps to keep your blend from deteriorating.

So: practise your carefully learned techniques, add some common sense, freshen up the pot pourri, check the warmth, the lights and the music, and away you go.

MASSAGE TECHNIQUES

Massage manuals are full of French terms such as effleurage and pettrisage (*see* Glossary). In plain English, the five massage techniques are: stroking, patting, knuckling, squeezing and rubbing.

Stroking

You've stroked the dog or the cat and know how much they like it. Massage strokes on people have a similar but even more marked effect. They should follow the following rules of technique: the aroma-masseur or -masseuse strokes in two ways, with a pulling or a pushing motion, and either way lightly or heavily.

Take the heart as the centre of the body. If the masseur is pulling or pushing towards the heart, she or he can use pressure. If stroking away from the heart, only the lightest touch should be used. Stroking should begin and end all massage sessions, and it should be used in between the other techniques.

Patting

This is the least used of the five. Patting with the fingertips gives light stimulation to small areas.

Knuckling

The hands are clenched in very light fists. Gentle circular movements are made using mainly the knuckles of the top joints of your fingers.

Squeezing

Squeezing and letting go, usually with both hands at once, is a powerful technique involving plenty of effort from the masseur and giving a clear effect on the subject.

Large muscles or muscle groups need more massage input than stroking can provide – in fact, 'need' is *almost* the right word, because the plunging, turning, squeezing, lifting and pressing actions of the bread-maker are the nearest equivalent to this deep form of massage, except that in massage the subject is human and expecting sympathetic treatment. Slow and kindly should be your kneading; no violence, please.

Rubbing

Everybody has, without knowing it was a massage technique, used friction, or rubbing, on a cold winter's day to warm their hands up. It's the same thing in massage: the harder and faster the masseur rubs, the better the results.

PRACTICAL USES OF AROMATHERAPY

The principal actions of aromatherapy oils are:

- as relaxants
- as tonics
- for aches and pains
- for skin care
- to induce sleep
- to create ambience
- to act as an aphrodisiac

Aromatic Relaxation

Stressed? Stress is the modern disease, accepted as an inevitable part of normal life, and so you allow stress to take its invisible toll of body and mind.

It may be, in a particular case, that there is little you can do about the causes of the stress, nor possibly even about the subject's ability to handle it, but you can do something to relieve the symptoms.

Aromatherapy is essentially a gentle way to improve well-being and restore proper functioning, using natural substances whose powers were studied and respected many centuries ago.

These days, the gentleness which is central to aromatherapy, combined with the therapeutic qualities offered by nature, produce a treatment for stress which is as harmonious as it is effective. Of course, nobody is suggesting you should be wandering around in a state of aromatic, spaced-out bliss the whole time. You need a bit of stress to spark you off, but too much causes fatigue and may shorten life expectancy.

Quite a number of essential oils are relaxants (*see* below) but several are pre-eminent among them, and these can be used singly or in combinations to suit you. This book is not going to examine the psychological roots of anybody's stress, which may indeed need to involve other forms of therapy; individuals may be predominantly depressed, or anxious, or a mixture of the two, or may confuse the two states. This book can only provide general guidelines for mood therapy. If at first you don't succeed, try another essential oil.

The oils most widely used and frequently commended for their virtues in relief of stress are those of lavender and sandalwood. Any first attempt to relax someone should be with one of these.

Also highly commended would be patchouli, sweet marjoram and vetivert from my second group of suggested oils (*see* page 54), plus chamomile from my Top Ten (*see* page 32).

Other oils with permutations of the right qualities include clary sage, frankincense, lemongrass, petitgrain and tangerine. Ylang ylang is also on the list but perhaps should be kept for special occasions, plus rose otto and true neroli if the stress is caused by being a millionaire (*see* aromatic sleep, below).

Blends can really be as simple or as complicated as you like, but simple ones are probably preferable. Were you to become an advanced student of aromatherapy you might investigate synergistic blends for the treatment of guilt, or conduct experiments into the best proportions of which six oils should be employed against helplessness and bewilderment. When things are as bad as that, perhaps a more fundamental, stringent treatment is required than aromatherapy's gentle benefits.

Meanwhile, you might like to deal with a case of old-fashioned 'nerves' by using a blend of equal amounts of lavender and vetivert. Alternatively, when the mood is gloomy, try lavender, chamomile and clary sage. If the stress in your subject tends to produce tense snappiness, then treat him or her to a massage of chamomile and sweet marjoram.

Aromatic Tonics

It's a cold, grey Sunday morning in late winter. You look out of the window at the fine but persistent drizzle and, through the depressing trickle of raindrops down the glass, you see the jobs that need doing in the garden. If this scene describes your general mood, you may only be showing the occasional sort of emotional and spiritual drain that everybody feels at one time or another.

Even more lowering is a pervasive mood of not being quite 'up to it'. You might have a frequent lack of vitality which means you look back at the day and close your eyes to avoid having to count the things you have left undone. Worst of all, you may feel that nobody loves you when you're down. You find a half-life of lying in bed that bit longer more attractive than the full life which awaits you after bouncing out of bed in the morning.

Aromatherapy is not going to bring you a sudden vision of the meaning of life, if you were wondering what on earth it was all for, but it can give you a lift and it can add some zest. Then, with your spirits brightened and your senses sharpened, you may well feel up to whatever it was, and once you've got up there and done it, maybe it won't be so difficult next time.

If you can't quite get to the seaside, but you want to experience the bracing effect of a breath of ozone, visit your aroma box instead and hope to find some or all of these essential oils which can be relied upon for bracing and uplifting those who are down in the mouth.

From my Top Ten (*see* below):

- eucalyptus, geranium, juniper, lemon balm or melissa, rosemary

Add, if you wish, for more interest and variety, some of these from the second shelf:

- basil, bergamot, lemon, peppermint.

For even more versatility, there are also:

- black pepper, cypress, ginger, grapefruit, orange, palmarosa.

Try cypress, geranium and grapefruit together, or eucalyptus, grapefruit and rosemary. Experiment also by adding one of the relaxer oils to two of the revivers, giving you a blend suitable for those times when you need the motivation of a pick-me-up but you also need your nerves steadying. For example, before a big occasion, try palmarosa and lemon with sandalwood, or bergamot and palmarosa with clary sage, or any of them with lavender.

Aromatics for aches and pains

There are as many pains as there are muscles and bones, and producing a comprehensive aromatherapy index for everything would require a much weightier volume than this one, and assume diagnostic skills not communicable via the written word.

Aches and pains have many and complicated causes, so let us stick here to a general approach, hoping to provide some relief where there is a problem, and some flexibility and a smile where there is stiffness and a grunt and a wince. To soothe our ills, we have at our disposal aromatic baths, massage, and a little battery of oils which will make life a bit more fun than it was.

A good general kit for **pain and stiffness** in muscles and joints would include:

- chamomile, eucalyptus, lavender, rosemary and sweet marjoram

More specifically, for **cramp**:

- chamomile, cypress, juniper, rosemary, sweet marjoram, tangerine

For **strains and sprains**:

- ginger, lavender, rosemary, sweet marjoram

For **rheumatic and arthritic pain**: where there is inflammation and swelling (be very gentle):

- chamomile, cypress, eucalyptus, juniper, lavender, lemon, rosemary

Where you need relaxing warmth, use:

- black pepper, ginger, sweet marjoram

For **bruises and knocks**:

- geranium, lavender, rosemary, cypress

Other oils with beneficial qualities in this area of treatment include:

- cajeput, naiouli and vetivert

Aromatic Skin Care

This book is not going to claim that your eczema, psoriasis or chronic acne – which so far has defeated the best of modern medical science – is miraculously curable by aromatherapy. However, these conditions can be eased by using essential oils in conjunction with pharmaceutical products.

The cosmetic side of skin care is dealt with more fully in the section on beauty treatments. Meanwhile, for the general health and care of our outermost layers we can divide quite a large number of oils into categories matching the most common, everyday complaints which may not worry the doctor but do worry the sufferer.

For skin which is **dry, itchy, tired or sore**, you need the soothers and healers :

- chamomile, lavender, petitgrain, sandalwood, vetivert

For **oily skin, spots and skin in need of refreshment,** the antiseptics and tonics are:

- cypress, eucalyptus, geranium, juniper, lemon, rosemary

For **cuts, sores and bites**, the stronger, more medicinal oils are:

- cajeput, and – especially – tea tree.

Clary sage, lemongrass, palmarosa and patchouli also have particular benefits in skin care.

Aromatic Sleep

When asked to pick their top two oils for helping people get to sleep, most of the aromatherapists in the world would probably say chamomile and sweet marjoram, with split votes for lavender, sandalwood or ylang ylang as a best third.

If you find that these oils on their own are not doing a satisfactory job, try blending small and equal amounts – say two or three drops – of chamomile, lavender and ylang ylang, or mix lavender with vetivert, which has special qualities in this department. Other oils which may help are benzoin, clary sage and petitgrain.

We have not yet mentioned the essential oils available to those of us who worry about having too much money, rather than too little. If your lack of sleep is caused by the bumps made in the mattress by multiple wads of bank notes, buy yourself some oil of rose, or go completely mad, hang the expense, and buy true neroli as well.

To go outside our range of recommended oils for once, there is an oil made from the root of a common herb called valerian which is a specific for insomnia. Valerian has a very long tradition in herbal medicine and was a popular remedy for what was once called 'the vapours', a term covering a range of conditions from depression to hysteria.

Valerian root was also used around Tudor times to perfume clothes, although few people would thank you for that now. Cats like the smell, however, and will roll on valerian plants in the garden. The essential oil is more pleasant than the plant but it is less widely available than some, its only real use being in insomnia and nerve-calming.

Aromatic Aphrodisiacs

Let's be quite clear about this. There are no secret essential oils with magic qualities. There is nothing in the aroma shop which can be slipped into the lover's wine, sprinkled on sleeping eyelids or burned to perfume a boudoir, which will have the same level of effect as the princess' kiss on the frog. Cures for unrequited love are not in the catalogue. Physical impossibilities cannot be rendered possible. Youthful performance, if long gone, cannot be conjured up. However, if there is potential, we might be able to do something.

Experts agree that only one of my Top Ten oils is an aphrodisiac, and that is ylang ylang. Some of the other Top Ten oils are commended, if not unanimously – juniper berry, rosemary and sandalwood, for example – and others have romantic attributes which can be employed as part of a multi-tactic strategy.

Several of my second group of oils can be regarded in a similarly positive light to ylang ylang, for instance clary sage, ginger, and lemon. Others with general stimulant or soothing properties can be helpful in the right context.

Two oils with very firm reputations as encouragers of romantic feelings are prohibitively expensive. The rich may be able to afford rose and jasmine, but the rest of us have ylang ylang at our disposal, and fortunately there is little difference as far as results are concerned.

If you must have rose, you can make the sacrifice seem less by buying it diluted and ready for use in a carrier oil. Alternatively, you can simulate the aroma – if not the qualities – of rose with a mixture of ylang ylang and clary sage.

Recipes for romantic blending are given below. Of course, you can create your own blends, and you can alter the balance of the blends given according to special circumstances.

Check on the other qualities of the oils as given below before you experiment too wildly.

Oils to drop hints with: a little subterfuge can go a long way, such as a drop of oil carefully placed where the desired one will surely find it. Give him or her a present, but make sure there's a scrap of cotton or tissue in the packing on which you have 'accidentally' tipped a minute quantity of oil.

Next time it's the birthday of the object of desire, or Valentine's Day, don't forget the aromatic clue inside the greetings card. Considering the price of cards, you might not want to use jasmine or rose, but geranium or ylang ylang should do the job just as well.

Oils for the right atmosphere: whether it's just a drink or two in the sitting room or a lovingly prepared six-course meal, romantic inclinations can be identified and developed by a subtle atmosphere containing the most suitable aromas. A couple of bowls of pot pourri might be inkling enough, or you might want to intimate rather more emphatically with a burner.

In either case, the oils to use include benzoin, patchouli and ylang ylang. Add one of the citrus oils such as grapefruit if some waking up needs to be done, or add sandalwood for a relaxing note.

Males with amorous intentions might add clary sage or black pepper. Females could try chamomile and palmarosa.

Should you be past the drinks and dinner stage and wanting simply to make sure that the bedroom is not only for sleeping, a good blend for the bedside pot pourri uses palmarosa as the base – say 10 drops – with a couple of drops each of ylang ylang and clary sage. If you can get them, you might also add a similar amount of nutmeg and lime.

If you are exhausted by all this secret aromatic activity, feeling full after the six courses or tired and emotional after too many glasses of wine, you could consider a nice warm bath to get you back into the mood. Grapefruit, palmarosa and, again, ylang ylang suggest themselves.

Oils for close encounters: one school of thought says that it is the massage that has the effect. Romantic conclusions would, they say, inevitably follow the stroking and squeezing, even if you used a blend of virgin olive and tea tree. Such people are cynical in the extreme and do not deserve magic moments.

Massage, of course, is all part and parcel, but it is far, far better to use a blend of oils designed for the purpose. As with all massage, the right essential oils with it increase the effect beyond simple addition.

Make a blend of equal amounts of lemon and palmarosa, five drops each, plus a drop or two of ylang ylang. Alternatively, use tangerine as the base, with black pepper added to it.

Oils to fuel the drives: if the idea is not so much to catch and kiss, but to make the already-caught want to kiss again, the classic sex drive oils are clary sage, geranium and ylang ylang, or even rose otto, if you deem it worth the expense. How you use them is up to you.

THE TOP TEN OILS

In alphabetical order, the top ten essential oils are:
•chamomile •cypress •eucalyptus •geranium
•juniper •lavender •rosemary •sandalwood
•tea (ti) tree •ylang ylang

Of these, only chamomile is expensive, although juniper berry and best sandalwood are also dearer than the other seven. This is a basic beginner's list of safe oils which covers a variety of the most common purposes.

Chamomile

Uses: as a relaxer; for aches and pains; for skin care; for inducing sleep.

Safe, versatile and held in highest regard for thousands of years, chamomile is one of the most important oils of all.

Nowadays, you will see two or even three kinds of chamomile on sale: Roman, German and Maroc. Which do you use?

Roman and German are very similar. German is less common and more expensive with a stronger blue colour. Its one advantage over Roman is possibly some extra power against skin complaints and so it tends to be used when the severity of the complaint justifies the extra expense.

Maroc is a relative newcomer. Strictly speaking, it is not chamomile at all except by common name. It is disregarded by some experts because it does not have as many uses and may not have such a powerful effect as Roman or German chamomile. However, it is cheaper and quite similar, and should be found effective with skin problems and as a relaxer and reliever of tensions.

Roman chamomile, *Chamaemelum nobile*, also called sweet, English, garden and true chamomile, is the one of chamomile lawn fame. It has a daisy-like flower, ferny leaves and a sharp apple scent. Chamomile is not only good for people. Also called the 'Plant Doctor', it is supposed to help the growth and well-being of the other plants in the garden just by being there.

The oil is distilled from the flowers and is middle note (*see* Glossary).

Chamomile for relaxation

Effective to a certain extent in all kinds of emotional and stressful conditions, chamomile is especially commended as a calming substance. When someone is upset by a traumatic experience, feeling they can't cope with life, suffering with 'nerves' or stress, this oil can be most helpful.

Its usefulness as a calming agent combines well with its anti-inflammatory and mild pain-killing properties (*see* aches and pains below) in such problems as infant teething troubles. Try chamomile in the child's bath, or in an aroma ring in the nursery.

Obviously, any sort of pain or physical irritation will negatively affect the sufferer's mood. Both problems can be eased by chamomile.

Suitable methods for relaxing with chamomile: water; applicators; vaporisers; massage

Chamomile for aches and pains

Its ability to reduce inflammation is one of the most prized features of this many-sided oil. It is also credited with a gentle analgesic effect and so many uses can be suggested where muscles and joints are swollen and causing distress. Rheumatic and arthritic sufferers can look to chamomile for relief, as can children and adults with much more short-term complaints, such as tiredness after exertion.

Next time you walk those few extra miles further than you thought, try chamomile in a foot bath. What could be more pleasant than a chamomile massage after a vigorous work-out? Perhaps the first gardening week-end of the year has stiffened muscles which are not so young as they were? Chamomile will help here too.

Methods for using chamomile for aches and pains: water; applicators; massage

Chamomile for skin care
Anti-inflammatory, gentle, soothing, antiseptic, able to give some relief from pain – this is obviously a good combination for skin which is sore from being wet and cold.

Chamomile may also help with teenage spots, dry skin, windburn, sunburn, or even chronic skin conditions such as acne and psoriasis. A chamomile compress can be used to take the soreness out of a boil, a minor wound or burn, or an insect bite.

Methods for using chamomile in skin care:
applicators; massage

Chamomile for inducing sleep
Along with lavender and some of my second group of oils, chamomile is one of the most frequently recommended oils for sleepless nights. It must be used sparingly, because too much can have the opposite effect. It is safe for children.

Methods for inducing sleep:
water; applicators; vaporisers; massage

Chamomile for use in digestive complaints
Changes in diet bring about a whole range of problems, from constipation to diarrhoea, from heartburn to flatulence. Chamomile can help in all such unpleasant situations, and while there is no known cure for a hangover, at least the world seems a less oppressive place with chamomile aromatherapy.

Methods for easing digestive complaints: water; applicators; vaporisers; massage

Chamomile for menstrual problems
Chamomile, along with geranium from my top ten, does seem to have special properties for the relief of the pains and stresses associated in some women with periods, pre-menstrual tension and menopausal problems. Its calming and muscle-relaxing powers combine to relieve such cases.

Methods for menstrual problems: water; vaporisers; applicators

Chamomile as an aphrodisiac
Roman chamomile is classed as a feminine scent. Although not widely used as a liquid ingredient by perfume manufacturers, try it by the vaporising methods or in pot pourri to give a feminine touch.

Cypress

Uses: as a reviver; for aches and pains; skin care

Cypress is chiefly known as an astringent, deodorant, drying oil. It can also be good for circulatory, digestive and menopausal problems.

Safe and unlikely to cause any irritation, cypress oil has a very long history, going back with myrrh and frankincense to ancient Babylon. In Far Eastern tradition, cypress is considered a useful aid when fluid is the problem, such as heavy sweating, heavy loss of menstrual fluid, diarrhoea.

Cupressus sempervirens is not grown much in the United Kingdom as it requires warmer climes. You will see a lot of it in the south of France, where it is grown widely for commercial use.

The oil is distilled from the twigs, needles and cones and is middle note (*see* Glossary). Cypress is widely used in men's toiletries because its 'heavy' scent can be more acceptable for men than the floral oils.

Cypress as a tonic

Cypress is a good mind-clearer and can help when a pick-me-up is needed, or when the brain is buzzing and you can't sleep.

Methods for cypress as a tonic: water; vaporisers; massage

Cypress for aches and pains

Again, this is not its main use, but cypress can be put to beneficial use with cramps and swellings. Where poor circulation is causing the discomfort, this oil should be especially helpful.

Methods for aches and pains: water; applicators; massage

Cypress for skin care

All essential oils are antiseptic in some way but cypress especially so. Cypress is also an astringent and can be used as a styptic to stop blood, although it is chiefly for its fragrance that perfume manufacturers use it so much in aftershave. Cypress is a skin revitaliser and freshener, and is particularly employed against greasy, oily skin.

Method for skin care: applicators

Cypress as an aphrodisiac
Cypress is of limited use in this respect; it is more likely to make you think of a bracing walk in January than of romantic evenings in tropical moonlight.

Eucalyptus

Uses: as a tonic; for aches and pains; for skin care

It is widely used to combat breathing problems, both the bronchial and asthmatic sorts. Anyone who has ever had a cold will surely recognise this celebrated cold treatment, one of the most powerful-smelling ingredients in chest and head-clearing ointments, inhalants and in cough sweets.

There are something like 500 varieties of eucalyptus. The one used most for commercial essential oil is *Eucalyptus globulus*, which is the famous blue gum tree of Australia. The oil is distilled from the leaves and is top note.

Eucalyptus as a tonic
Feeling sleepy? Don't want to feel sleepy? Few essential oils can clear the fuzz away like eucalyptus. It can also give relief on a muggy, hot day.

Methods for eucalyptus as a tonic:
water; applicators; vaporisers; massage

Eucalyptus for aches and pains
Like quite a number of essential oils, eucalyptus can be helpful with general pains and swellings, but its main strength is in providing relief and respite for tired, over-worked muscles. This is the one for post-aerobic stiffening, or for pulls and strains.

Methods for aches and pains: water; applicators; massage

Eucalyptus for skin care
Eucalyptus is one of the stronger antiseptics among essential oils, and its cooling, anti-inflammatory, insect-repelling properties make it a natural choice for stings and bites, rashes, flushed skin and spots.

Method for skin care: applicators

Eucalyptus for aiding breathing
Coughs, colds, throat infections, catarrh, 'flu, blocked sinus, asthma – all such constrictions and congestions can be relieved with eucalyptus. The antiseptic action may help clear away some conditions, and the invigorating vapours will make you feel better.

Methods for aiding breathing: water; vaporisers; massage

Eucalyptus as an aphrodisiac
Eucalyptus tends to have practical uses such as

dissolving oily substances, rather than stirring romantic notions. However, its harmonising nature can help cool overheated emotions in conflict.

Geranium

Uses: as a tonic; for skin care

Geranium can be good for pre-menstrual tension or menopausal problems. A very popular all-round oil, geranium, or more properly, pelargonium, has a scent which almost everybody finds highly attractive. It is a safe, uplifting, body-cleansing oil with a long tradition through its wild equivalents, herb Robert and cranesbill.

Although these have many specific uses in herbal lore, for example in cures for dandruff, sterility and peptic ulcers, geranium oil in family aromatherapy is most important for its ability to lighten the mood and to help with skin care.

Pelargonium graveolens is the geranium used for oil extraction, one of many hundreds of varieties bred from the African original since it was brought to Europe 300 years ago. The essential oil is distilled mainly from the leaves and is middle note.

Geranium as a tonic

You've see those television advertisements suggesting you should take such and such a pill to relieve your tense, nervous headache? Instead, use geranium oil. When the day has given you a battering and your spirits need a lift, this is the one that should be used.

Methods for geranium as a tonic: water; applicators; vaporisers; massage

Geranium for skin care

This is a cleansing, toning, sharpening oil and so is helpful with those problems which come with greasy, over-oily skin. It can help you deal with cold sores, chilblains and weather-beaten skin. Used as a gargle, just a couple of drops in warm water, geranium has a soothing effect on sore mouths and throats.

Methods for skin care: water; applicators

Geranium as an aphrodisiac

Geranium is classed by perfumers as both a male and a female-attracting scent and is recommended for stimulating hormone production. Some experts say it can be helpful where certain urges don't seem to be quite so urgent any more, but in any case its lively, flowery smell can only act positively in a romantic situation.

Juniper

Uses: as a tonic; for aches and pains; for skin care; as an aphrodisiac.

The berries and the rest of this evergreen shrub are used in oil production, but the superior product is the one distilled just from the berry, which is the same berry that is used to flavour gin. Juniper berry oil is middle note (*see* Glossary).

Juniper oil is mainly regarded as a cleanser and stimulator. It was used for centuries as a household disinfectant and in herbal remedies to stimulate bowel and kidney action. Along with the related cypress, and eucalyptus, this oil can be useful when detoxification is needed.

WARNING: although safe in most situations, juniper must not be used by pregnant women, especially in the early months, nor on anyone with kidney trouble. In any case it should never be used over-liberally although there will usually be no problems with a sensible approach.

Juniper as a tonic

This is a good pick-me-up, an uplifting oil in times of stress and anxiety. Tiredness, lassitude and general 'floppiness' can be dispelled. If you are changing your lifestyle habits and resolving to follow a healthy regime, then juniper and the New You definitely go together.

Methods for juniper as a tonic: water; applicators; vaporisers; massage

Juniper for aches and pains

Used in the herbal tradition for gout, arthritis and rheumatism, juniper stimulates circulation and gives a fillip to aching muscles and creaking joints. Period pains and aching breasts can also be relieved.

Methods for aches and pains: water; applicators; massage

Juniper for skin care
Oily skin, greasy hair, spots and tired skin should all respond well to juniper. This is a tonic, strong on the healthy glows and the feel-good factor. It is used in the toiletry industry as an ingredient in the spicier after-shaves and perfumes.

Methods for skin care: applicators

Juniper as an aphrodisiac
Juniper as a perfume ingredient is supposed to be attractive to both males and females, and some experts, although not all, give it as an aphrodisiac. More experiments are obviously needed.

Lavender

Uses: as a relaxant; for aches and pains; for skin care; to induce sleep

It can also be good for digestive and menstrual or menopausal problems, helpful in colds and flu, blocked sinuses and sore throats, and is an insect repellent.

This is the most versatile oil, the best all-rounder and the one you cannot be without. It is safe, and has been used in the herbal tradition for thousands of years as a virtual cure-all and general comforter, although especially as a pain killer, healer of wounds, and as a balancer of the spirits. Lavender is credited with both calming and uplifting powers and so can be equally prescribed as a soothing agent in anxiety and a stimulant in depression.

As with chamomile and sandalwood, the Latin name is important for making sure you are buying the oil of the right plant. *Lavendula angustifolia*, also called *Lavendula officinalis*, is true lavender, of which there are several species with mauve, purple or blue flowers, all of which can be used to make the oil by distillation.

Lavender oil is middle note. Oils from spike lavender, or from lavendin – a cross between lavender and spike lavender – have wide uses similar to those of true lavender but their more medicinal, moth-ballish scent makes them less widely acceptable.

Lavender for relaxation

Emotions can be upset in many ways, through a continuing situation such as environment or an on-going relationship, or a more sudden cause. The result can be to send the sufferer in the direction of hysteria and panic, or towards depressive headaches, morose lack of self-belief and a defeatist attitude. Lavender is a balancing oil, one which tends to bring you back to normal from whichever direction, and so can be described as an energiser and a calming agent.

Methods for lavender as a relaxant: water; applicators; atmospherics; massage

Lavender for aches and pains

Lavender's therapeutic qualities have always been

believed to include pain relief and reduction of inflammation, and so this oil obviously suggests itself for dealing with muscular strains and shock.

Stiff joints, headaches and period pains can also be susceptible to its aromatic powers.

Methods to relieve aches and pains: water; applicators; vaporisers; massage

Lavender for skin care
This oil in the herbal tradition is said to encourage cell growth and so should be used to help with mending and regeneration in all kinds of skin ailments: bites, stings, boils, burns, stretch marks, rashes, spots, cold sores. It is also recommended against athlete's foot.

Methods for skin care: water; applicators; massage

Lavender to induce sleep
When grandmother puts a few drops of lavender perfume on a handkerchief and leaves it under her pillow, she is following one of the oldest remedies for insomnia in the world. She also, without knowing it perhaps, has the dose right. You just need to use a very little of the essential oil otherwise it can begin to work as a stimulant.

Methods for using lavender to induce sleep: water; vaporisers

Lavender as an aphrodisiac
Another oil whose perfume is classified as both a male and female fragrance, lavender does not

number 'aphrodisiac' among its many characteristics nor, like some, is it expected to reawaken desire.

However, it does have a very pleasant, gentle, peaceful and healing aroma. Possibly it might aid romance when it's time to kiss and make up.

Rosemary

Uses: as a tonic; for aches and pains; for skin care; as an aphrodisiac

It can also be good for digestive problems, is helpful with impeded breathing, is an insect repellent and is highly regarded in hair care. Rosemary is one of the most important oils among our top ten. As long as humans have used medicine, rosemary has been employed for its antiseptic, cleansing, clearing powers and it has been claimed that it also aids memory and concentration.

Interestingly, while modern users of rosemary stalks throw them on the barbecue for extra savour, the ancient Greeks used to burn them as tributes to the gods. Mediaeval Europeans thought it would drive away evil spirits.

Besides rosemary's range of qualities in skin care, it is also recommended particularly for getting rid of dandruff and livening up tired, dull hair.

Rosemary's flowering sprigs are used to make the oil, which is middle note.

Although generally safe, rosemary must not be used by pregnant women, especially in the early months, nor by anyone with epilepsy.

Rosemary as a tonic

This stimulating oil works like sunshine on a misty morning, clearing away mental fogs and sharpening fuzzy minds. If you don't feel quite up to an especially busy day ahead, try a few drops of rosemary oil in the morning bath, and likewise if there's a hectic evening to enjoy after a very wearing day.

Methods for rosemary as a tonic: water; vaporisers; massage

Rosemary for aches and pains

Physical as well as mental uplift can be expected from rosemary and this fact, along with its mild pain-relieving and all-round livening effects, make it very good for aching muscles.

Methods for aches and pains: water; applicators; vaporisers; massage

Rosemary for skin care

Skin conditions which will respond to cleansing, antiseptic, astringent, stimulating action will be helped by rosemary. Where the flow of blood in the veins needs encouragement, and the skin needs a tonic, rosemary must come to mind.

Methods for skin care: water; applicators; massage

Rosemary as an aphrodisiac
It was used ceremonially to represent love and death in the ancient religions, which may be why some experts give it as an aphrodisiac. Certainly it would be more useful for wakening than creating a romantic, sensual background.Rosemary is classified as a masculine scent which is attractive to females.

Sandalwood

Uses: as a relaxant; for skin care; for inducing sleep

Sandalwood can also be good for digestive problems, and can help where coughs and bronchial infections have caused soreness.

Eucalyptus, rosemary and juniper are among the great stimulators, but sandalwood is one of the great calming agents, and safe, too. The familiar rich aroma has been present in perfumes for thousands of years. The herbal tradition has sandalwood especially effective in the treatment of ailments in the lungs and the bladder, and as a soother of digestive upsets including hiccups, heartburn and morning sickness.

According to the Bible, God spoke to King Solomon and instructed him to make his temple furniture of sandalwood, and unfortunately, its widespread use for construction purposes has lead to its near-extinction. Sandalwood oil is also used very widely in incenses and so the scent has strong associations with ceremony, serenity and wisdom.

There are two kinds of sandalwood oil on regular sale. Proper sandalwood is made from the wood of the parasitic evergreen tree *Santalum album*. This tree, which has to be at least 30 years old to produce the oil, comes from the province of Mysore in eastern India and is the more expensive of the two because it is so rare.

Sandalwood essential oil is base note (*see* Glossary). West Indian sandalwood, *Amyris balsamifera*, no botanical relation, is a cheaper, inferior substitute which is really only for burners and similar usage.

Sandalwood as a relaxant

Anyone who is anxious, tense, nervy, highly strung, or worried can benefit from the deeply affecting, calming powers of sandalwood. 'Sedative' is a word which has changed its meaning from the original ('making calm, allaying, assuaging'), now signifying a strong knock-out drug. Sandalwood is a sedative in the original sense of the word.

Methods for using sandalwood as a relaxant: water; applicators; vaporisers; massage

Sandalwood for skin care

This oil is chiefly a softener and a soother, so use it for dry skin, wrinkly skin, flaky skin, and where there is irritation from sunburn, nettle stings and so on. Itching and rawness, for instance from shaving or exposure to wind and rain, can be relieved with sandalwood.

Methods for skin care: applicators; massage

Sandalwood for inducing sleep
It really is one of the most attractive, well-rounded aromas to have in your bedroom. Sandalwood creates a serious, calm ambience, not a frivolous one, and this aspect of the oil may well help its natural sedative qualities towards easing troubled minds at night.

Methods: water; vaporisers; massage

Sandalwood as an aphrodisiac
Sandalwood is a two-sided perfume in the sexual sense, being attractive both to male and female, and is said to be able to induce passionate notions when otherwise they might not occur.

Its sweet, woody balsamic scent lends itself to attractive blends in perfume manufacture and for this reason sandalwood is often used as a base note – that is, one of the long-staying ingredients – in several leading brands of men's toiletry.

Tea Tree or Ti Tree

Uses: skin care

This small relative of the eucalyptus was given its name because the early settlers in Australia brewed its leaves to make a drink.

Tea tree oil is distilled from these leaves, and is top note. It is from the same botanical family as allspice – which produces an oil to be used occasionally and only with great care – and eucalyptus and cajeput, both popular oils.

Tea tree has applications in the treatment of many kinds of infection. The oil is an essential for your first-aid kit. It is a very strong antiseptic, much stronger, in fact, than carbolic, yet is perfectly safe even for people prone to allergic reactions.

Like eucalyptus, it is a cleanser and a healer and had been used thus for unmeasured time by the Australian aborigines before ever European settlers got hold of it.

It is the only essential oil credited by sceptics and aromatherapists alike with powers against all three invaders of human well-being: bacteria, viruses and fungi. Of course, it has no long herbal tradition in western medicine, but is now the subject of considerable interest among orthodox researchers.

Tea tree for skin care

This oil works against the causes of infection, swelling and eruption as well as reducing the symptoms, and so it is widely employed against sores, blisters, spots, rashes, verrucas and warts.

It is also effective against discomfort of interior skin, such as mouth ulcers and sore throats, and is so safe that it can be confidently employed to fight fungal infections such as vaginal thrush.

Methods for skin care: water; applicators

Tea tree in medicinal use

Coughs, catarrh and afflictions of the lungs and air passages; fevers; septic wounds; wherever you might use a conventional decongestant, antiseptic or cooling agent, tea tree can be your aid.

Methods for tea tree in medicinal use: water; applicators; vaporisers; massage

Ylang Ylang

Uses: as a relaxant; in skin care; to induce sleep; as an aphrodisiac

You should buy only 'Extra' or 'Grade 1' oils which are from the first distillations of the flowers.

The ylang ylang tree is native to Madagascar and the Philippines; it seems to be a bit of a one-off in the botanical world, and you would need the facilities and expertise of Kew Gardens to grow it in this country.

Widely used in the perfume industry for its exotic floral scent and its legendary aphrodisiac qualities, Ylang Ylang is an ingredient in some of the world's most famous and expensive concoctions.

Care has to be taken in its use. Although safe, the sheer intoxication of its scent can prove to be overwhelming and some people may get a headache or nausea as a result.

Ylang ylang for relaxation
This is a sedative oil. Anyone feeling that surge of anxiety which leads to an involuntary loss of cool can whisper 'Don't panic' to themselves as they unscrew the top of the Ylang Ylang.

It has excellent uses in personal relationships apart from the aphrodisiac. Ylang Ylang is a calmer of anger and frustration and so can be employed when such emotions might otherwise spoil something important. It is supposed also to help with conditions associated with anxiety such as high blood pressure and depression. It reassures and helps to build confidence.

Methods for ylang ylang as a relaxant: water; vaporisers; massage

Ylang ylang in skin care

Not its main use but may help with spots and minor skin ailments.

Methods for skin care: applicators; massage

Ylang ylang for inducing sleep

Gardens of flowers and dreamy summer scents can fill your bedroom when you sprinkle a few drops of ylang ylang on your pillow. It should also help induce a better quality of sleep, since it is promotes a speedy progression to the stage of rapid eye movement (REM), when creative or therapeutic dreaming may be experienced.

Methods: water; vaporisers; massage

Ylang ylang as an aphrodisiac

All the aromatherapy experts agree on this characteristic of ylang ylang, and so do the natives of the tropical Far East where it grows, among whom it is common custom to scatter the flowers on the bridal bed. It is said to work on both sexes although its strongly flowery scent makes it more feminine than masculine.

Methods for ylang ylang as an aphrodisiac: vaporisers; massage

SECONDARY OILS

The Top Ten oils listed above will provide the beginner with a basic aromatherapy set for most common purposes. In addition, you may wish to experiment with the following oils.

Basil

French or sweet basil, *Ocimum basilicum*, is the herb so popular in Italy and France for culinary use. The oil is a tonic: cooling, uplifting and restorative, and is highly regarded in the herbal tradition for its effects in respiratory ailments.

Safe, but not to be used during pregnancy, on young children, or anyone who is very ill.

Benzoin

In another form, oil of benzoin, made from the resin of the Asian tropical tree *Styrax benzoin*, is famous as friar's balsam. A balsam or balm is a healing, soothing substance, and the friar's type is especially for soothing respiratory complaints. Benzoin essential oil has this virtue, and is also good for the skin and as a warming relaxer.

It relieves stress and tension, aids depression and gives new hope to those with a sense of alienation from society. It gives confidence and helps emotional fatigue. Benzoin is a traditional ingredient in incense.

Safe, although can cause drowsiness, so do not use when driving or operating machinery. Masculine and feminine fragrance; base note (*see* Glossary).

Bergamot

If you have ever had Earl Grey tea, you will recognise oil of bergamot instantly. Made from the peel of the small, orange-like fruit of an Italian tree, *Citrus bergamia*, this is a cooling, uplifting, refreshing tonic of an oil, which is why it is frequently found in Eau de Cologne. Bergamot is also useful against coughs and colds, and skin problems.

Safe, but should not be used before going into or while in sunlight because this can cause it to stain and may also cause a rash.

Masculine and feminine fragrance; top note.

Black Pepper

As you might imagine, this oil – made from the whole peppercorns of the bush *Piper nigrum* – is the warming, rosy-glow type, so its sweet aroma can add mysterious depth to a blend.

Its main applications are aches and pains, colds, stiffness and chills, although it is also supposed to be good for heartburn, nausea, diarrhoea and loss of appetite.

For thousands of years, Chinese and Indian doctors have been using pepper for such stomach complaints. Emotionally, it can give stamina and vitality to someone who is apathetic and lethargic.

Safe, but be careful. Too much black pepper oil on the skin can cause severe irritation. Just a very little can be a masculine fragrance.

Black pepper oil is middle note (*see* Glossary).

Cajeput or Cajaput

This is the cheaper, Malaysian equivalent of eucalyptus and tea tree, but definitely third in the order of merit.

It has a narrower range of uses than the other two but is a powerful antiseptic and is used as such in some dental preparations, for example gargles and throat lozenges. Cajeput is also useful for a range of skin conditions such as oily skin and spots, or insect bites. It is good for stuffiness, head colds, muscular aches and pains and arthritis. It is also useful for respiratory complaints such as asthma, bronchitis and catarrh.

Safe, although may irritate sensitive skin and the mucous membranes.

Cedarwood B

This is the oil of the Virginian red cedar, *Juniperus virginiana*, the affordable near-equivalent of cedarwood A, *Cedrus atlantica*. Cedar is a Semitic word meaning 'the power of spiritual strength', and it is for long-standing conditions such as depression that cedarwood proves most useful.

The Amerindians used their red cedar as medicine against many ailments, but especially bronchial and rheumatic kinds.

This oil is regarded commercially as an insecticide and is good as a room freshener and insect repellent. Its ambient qualities can also be useful as an aid to meditation. Emotionally, it is useful for relaxing and soothing, or uplifting the spirits when a person is experiencing a lack of confidence.

Safe, but not to be used during pregnancy.
Masculine and feminine fragrance; base note.

Citronella

Cymbopogon nardus is a lemon-scented grass, related to the lemongrass used in eastern cookery, which also provides a useful oil (*see* below). Citronella essential oil is a powerful insecticide and deodorant. In aromatherapy it is generally used as a freshener and stimulator; it can clear the stale fog from heads and rooms equally well.

Generally safe but do not use using pregnancy.

Clary Sage

This is one with which to experiment carefully, not because it is toxic, but because it can do similar sorts of things to you as alcohol – and its effects can vary from person to person. It may make you feel good, it may make you feel sleepy or amorous. *Salvia sclarea* makes a cooling, anti-inflammatory oil which has a wide range of uses especially in skin care and throat infections, and in nervous stress where it seems to be able both to soothe and uplift.

Do not use during pregnancy, nor when you would normally avoid alcohol, such as when driving or operating machinery. It should not be used by people who suffer from high blood pressure. It may also cause problems for some women on the contraceptive pill or hormone replacement therapy. Clary sage is classed as both a feminine and masculine scent but much more employed in men's toiletries; top note.

Fennel

Sweet fennel is the tall, ferny, hardy herb with the aniseed flavour. Florence fennel is the close relative grown for its vegetable root. Both are varieties of *Foeniculum vulgare*, a plant with an enormous reputation from medieval times onwards.

Modern babies have it in gripe water, and the essential oil, made from the seeds, has aromatherapy uses mostly associated with digestive problems including hiccups, nausea, flatulence and constipation. Fennel is also associated with respiratory ailments such as asthma and bronchitis as well as circulatory disorders and muscular pain.

Safe in moderation; however, it is not to be used in pregnancy or by epileptics.

Frankincense

Cynics might think that the three wise men would have been better bringing gold, fennel and myrrh, but the oil made from the resin of the frankincense tree, *Boswellia carteri*, had religious significance well before that time, as an incense and as an agent for encouraging the right atmosphere for meditating on deep matters. This property is enhanced by the fact that it deepens and slows the breath. The ancients also used it for skin diseases and as a cosmetic rejuvenator, and this is possibly one of its main virtues today. It is also useful for easing period pains.

Frankincense can be good in clearing up colds and stuffiness and, allied to its old religious uses, as a calming influence in stress and anxiety.

Generally safe. Appealing to males and females; base note (*see* Glossary).

Ginger

The uses for the essence of the root of *Zingiber officinale* are no surprise; it is a warming, stimulating, livening-up kind of oil, widely employed against aches and pains, cramps, stiffness, poor circulation and tiredness.

The old doctors also knew about its qualities as a digestive aid, and old wives would have told their daughters how quickly it gets rid of morning sickness. It's a great pity that such ordinary but truly useful knowledge is not passed on so automatically as it once was.

Generally safe, but may be slightly phototoxic to some people, that is to say that it may cause skin irritation when exposed to sunlight. Classified as a masculine and a feminine fragrance; middle note (*see* Glossary). Use with caution because oil of ginger's reputation for warming, stimulating and livening is not confined to aches and pains. Be prepared for its effects on the romantic instincts.

Grapefruit

Citrus paradisi is thought of as a fruit of the morning, a starter for breakfast because it's a tonic, because it's high in vitamin C and because it helps digestion, especially of fatty foods. Aromatherapy gives it similar attributes – a tonic for the nerves and for the skin, a help in chills and colds, and to be included in massage blends where the subject has inches to spare.

Safe, but as with other citrus oils, do not use before going into sunlight, as it may stain the skin or cause an unpleasant skin reaction. Grapefruit oil will not keep as long as most oils, having a shelf life of about six months. Not a commercial perfume nor an aphrodisiac, but its euphoric qualities may help to brighten up a jaded heart and cope with feelings of resentment and envy.

Lemon

The essential oil of *Citrus limonum* is, like that of grapefruit, expressed from the skin of the fruit and, like grapefruit, is a tonic high in vitamin C. The lemon has a longer and more celebrated history, however, and is very highly regarded as a medicinal power in many kinds of infection and gastric upset.

Perhaps skin care is its major use in aromatherapy; it can be used against all sorts of swellings and wounds and as a rejuvenator.

It is also useful for headaches and to counteract feelings of resentment and bitterness.

Safe, although may stain the skin under ultraviolet light and/or cause a rash. Used commercially in masculine and feminine fragrances; top note.

Lemon Balm *see* Melissa

Lemongrass

The culinary variety of cymbopogen, C. *citratus*, is credited with rather more abilities than its relation citronella (*see* above). Its background in old Indian medicine is similar – anti-fever, anti-infection – and it is an insecticide, but in addition, lemongrass is a sedative.

Helpful in skin care, for clearing heads and lungs and for loosening and easing stiff muscles, this oil can additionally be beneficial with stress and nervous tension.

Generally safe, although some people might find it an irritant. Masculine fragrance; top note (*see* Glossary).

Mandarin *see* Tangerine

Marjoram

There are two kinds of essential oil with this name – sweet marjoram, *Origanum majorana*, and Spanish marjoram, *Thymus mastichina*. Sweet marjoram does everything the Spanish one does, such as soothing aches and pains, bruises and strains. It is also especially recommended for insomnia, and for its deeply affecting ability to smooth away troubles and comfort the poor in spirit, such as those suffering from recent grief or bereavement. Spanish marjoram or oregano is not really marjoram at all; it just smells like it.

Sweet marjoram is generally safe, but should not be used during pregnancy. While classifying it as an ingredient suitable for both masculine and feminine fragrances, perfume manufacturers may be interested to know that sweet marjoram (along with oil of hops) is supposed to be a sexual turn-off and is therefore recommended as a cure for over-powerful sex drives. The ancients believed it could console the bereaved and bring peace of mind to the frantic, but they never prescribed it for wedding nights.

Melissa or Lemon Balm

This is the oil that cheers. Used in herbal medicine from the very beginnings of the art, one of its common names is Heart's Delight and here is where its value lies. The old doctors, knowing nothing of psychiatry but recognising melancholy, anxiety and loss of confidence, used melissa to breathe new life into a flagging spirit.

Although it also has some therapeutic value, particularly in skin and digestive disorders, oil of melissa is kept mainly as a general tonic, or specifically to help those prone to nervousness, loss of concentration, or the feeling that they are losing their battle with the world.

Safe. Lemon balm, *Melissa officinalis*, is usually sold in a form containing some citronella, lemon or lemongrass.

Myrrh

Egyptian mummies were embalmed using myrrh, but its cleansing, drying and warming properties are rather more useful these days for treating wounds, abrasions, and especially soreness in the mouth. Coughs and stuffiness can respond well to oil of myrrh, and it is said to be effective against fungal infections such as thrush and athlete's foot.

Safe but not to be used during pregnancy. Used as a base note in masculine and feminine fragrances.

Neroli or Orange Blossom

True neroli, made from the twice-yearly blossom of the Chinese orange-flower tree *Citrus aurantium amara*, is also truly expensive like rose and jasmine. Brides might consider it worth it, when they learn that this flower has a long romantic tradition linked to its emotional effects; it gives a feeling of peace although it also livens the spirits, and for this reason it was considered in many eastern folk traditions to be an essential component in wedding bouquets and bridal suite decoration.

Neroli oil is a skin tonic, and an emotional tonic too – in fact, its main employment is in relief of nervous tension, stress, including pre-menstrual tension, insomnia, shock and fear. It is reputed to aid the development of self-esteem and promote confidence. It has a wonderful aroma, of course, and the distillation by-product, orange flower water, has always been a popular skin refresher, culinary ingredient and perfume.

More widely obtainable and much, much cheaper is neroli B, a blend of oils made from close relatives in the aurantia family.

Generally safe, although the distilled oil may cause skin irritation. Used by perfumers in both masculine and feminine fragrances as a top note.

Niaouli

Definitely not to be confused with neroli, this is the Australian equivalent of cajeput, another antiseptic tea tree relative. It has been used by native peoples for many years as a purifier, healer and cleanser and as a warming easer of sore muscles. It is also used in respiratory conditions such as asthma, bronchitis and coughs.

Safe. The oil of *Melaleuca viridiflora* is a pharmaceutical ingredient in mouth-care and throat-care products.

Orange, Sweet

From the original Chinese native orange *Citrus sinensis* we now have navels, Jaffas, Valencias, Sevilles, and essential oil of orange.

Herbal doctors use orange for chest complaints and as a stimulant for appetite and digestion. In aromatherapy too the oil is recommended for the bronchial system and for upset stomachs, but is mainly used as a tonic in depression and nervousness. It can help to enliven sallow skin.

The oil made by pressing the ripe peel – which usually comes from Brazil – is safe and of better quality than the distilled kind. There is some confusion about whether this oil can irritate the skin in sunlight like some of the other citrus oils do, so use with care.

Classed as a masculine fragrance; top note.

Palmarosa

A relative of lemongrass and citronella, palmarosa – *Cymbopogon martini* – is very good for moisturising the skin and encouraging a bright and lively complexion.

It is also valued as an appetite stimulant and a tonic for tired spirits, being a gentle, comforting oil. Its cooling quality can counteract feelings of anger and jealousy.

Safe. Feminine fragrance; middle note (*see* Glossary for definition).

Patchouli

The aroma evokes tropical spices, warmth and calm, and one of its most commonplace uses is as a fragrance for bed linen where it has a dual function, being reputed to act as a stimulant to the creative urges as well as a stay-freshener.

In aromatherapy it is mainly commended for skin care, both to treat damaged and tired skin and to prevent infection, and for easing of stress. In the herbal tradition, *Pogostemon cablin*, or patchouli, is used to treat headaches and stomach complaints.

Safe. Use as a base note in both masculine and feminine fragrances.

Peppermint

Digestion, anything to do with coughs and colds, nausea, including morning sickness and, of course, minty freshness – these have been the work of peppermint for ever and a day.

If you can disassociate yourself from the toothpaste tube and the chewing gum packet, oil of peppermint can also be helpful as a cooling, invigorating agent and where muscles and skin need an oil with cleansing and anti-inflammatory properties. It is useful for digestive disturbance such as stomach cramps, nausea and flatulence.

Emotionally, the oil combats fatigue and aids clear thinking. It may also provide a calming effect to those suffering from feelings of anger, nervousness or shyness.

Generally safe, although it contains a lot of menthol, which can irritate some skin types. Some authorities suggest it should be avoided during pregnancy and while breast-feeding. Classed as a top-note masculine fragrance (*see* Glossary for definition).

Mentha piperita is true peppermint. *Mentha arvensis*, cornmint or peppermint B, is a slightly cheaper substitute with a higher menthol content.

Petitgrain

Widely thought of as a much cheaper substitute for neroli and made from the leaves and twigs of the same tree, *Citrus aurantium amara*.

Petitgrain is mainly employed in aromatherapy as a soothing agent in skin care, stress and insomnia.

It should also be considered in cases where the objective of the aromatherapy is to restore the body or emotions to their normal equilibrium, as for example in convalescence or any kind of shock to the system.

Safe. A top/middle note in feminine and masculine fragrances (*see* Glossary) but probably more masculine; an ingredient in several of the world's best-selling men's toiletries.

Rosewood

Distilled from the timber of the Amazonian hardwood tree *Aniba rosaedora*, this is a mild, general purpose oil for which most home therapists could easily find a substitute. Polish grandma's rosewood dining table, buy lavender oil for your aroma box instead of rosewood and do your bit for the rainforest. Rosewood is also available in synthetic form, which is used in cosmetic skin care, for minor wounds and for colds and coughs.

Safe. Masculine and feminine fragrance, middle/top note.

Tangerine

Often used with children, the elderly and pregnant women because of its safe and mild action in digestive complaints, especially those common physical disorders which have nervous origins such as hiccups. Tangerine is also good for jumpiness. Tangerine and mandarin oils are recommended for calming functions: sleeplessness, nervous tension and muscular cramps and spasms.

Generally safe, although like the other citrus oils, may cause skin irritation, especially when exposed to sunlight. Mandarin, *Citrus reticulata*, is more frequently used in commercial perfumery than tangerine, *Citrus madurensis*. Both are masculine and feminine fragrance, middle/top note.

Vetivert

Deeply relaxing, soothing and smoothing, this essence of the roots of *Vetiveria zizanoides*, which is related to lemongrass, has the highest reputation for bringing about tranquillity where there was storm and sleep where there was restlessness.

It has physical uses too, relaxing and easing tired and tense muscles and as a gentle help with skin roughness and soreness.

Safe. Its woody, smoky base note is included in masculine and feminine fragrances.

And all the others?

Caraway, cardamom, hyssop, jasmine, rose and rose otto, sage, tagetes, tonka bean, verbena . . . from allspice and amyris to valerian and violet, there are scores more oils which you could use, and scores – such as bitter almond, wintergreen and wormwood, which you should use on no account.

Most of the beneficial oils mentioned have uses in parallel with more widely obtainable oils, or are very expensive. Some can have specific applications in unusual cases which qualified aromatherapists would know about and which the most interested amateurs can study in more comprehensive and scholarly works than this.

We have listed a Top Ten as a starting point, and a second group of the most popular of the rest which you can try and add to your increasing armoury of knowledge and equipment.

The important thing always to remember is that essential oils are highly concentrated and not to be treated lightly. If something is not recommended you can be sure there is a good reason for it. Within the bounds of safety and care there is a lot of fun to be had and much useful work to be done.

AROMATHERAPY FOR DIFFERENT LIFESTYLES

Certain oils are particularly beneficial to specific conditions, lifestyles and ages, and can also be blended to provide special physical and emotional relief and enhance your quality of life.

Hair care and the body beautiful

Aromatherapy can help you make the most of what you've got, in the same way as washing the car does. A cleaner car may not be a better car, but it certainly looks as if it is.

Actually, that's not quite true. Aromatherapy can do more for you than a mere wash. It can help also with clearing away some of the more dispiriting malfunctions of the system such as spots and dandruff – and if it can't make you better looking as such, it can at least make you feel and look younger.

Starting with hair: essential oils can assist with the problems of dandruff, dry hair, greasy hair, or lifeless hair.

For dandruff in lank, greasy hair, try a blend of cedarwood, juniper, lemon and rosemary, 3 drops of each in 20 ml/1¼ tbsps of carrier oil. Massage well into the hair and scalp, and leave for an hour or more, shampoo with a gentle brand, then for a final rinse let your hair soak in water which has a drop of each of those oils in it.

Use the same method for dandruff in dry hair, but use different oils. These should be geranium, lavender and sandalwood, possibly with added chamomile, in the same proportions as above.

The same oils carried in a mixture of jojoba and almond oils, perhaps with some evening primrose added, will make a good conditioner for dry hair. Try using the mixture warm – heat it in a bottle in a cup of hot water – and leave it on the hair for 15 minutes, then shampoo as usual.

For greasy hair, add basil and cypress to the list given for dandruff in lank, greasy hair. Lavender and rosemary will give hair a shine, and cypress, lemon and rosemary together will give it a lift.

A good general tonic for the hair and scalp features cedarwood, rosemary and ylang ylang, 2 drops each, plus a drop of melissa. Pour out a small measure of vodka and stir the oils into it. Dilute with a little water and rub the result gently into the scalp.

Whatever your skin type, if your complexion is sallow, dull and lifeless and you want to improve its vitality, tone and texture, then a half dozen or so essential oils will be sufficient.

These are the oils that go with the skin types:

- **Greasy skin**: bergamot, juniper, lemon, ylang ylang
- **Dry skin:** chamomile, geranium, palmarosa, ylang ylang
- **Sensitive skin:** chamomile, neroli

To apply these oils to your skin you might like to make up a toner or a moisturiser. Add the oils, 1 or 2 drops to 50 ml/3¼ tbsps, to bottled water or to something more fragrant, such as rosewater.

To make a moisturising cream, add in the same proportions to a neutral base. Whatever your skin type, if it is suffering a temporary phase of seeming dull and lifeless, petitgrain is said to be able to restore your natural balance.

Spots of course are the plague of the young, although the tendency to spots can last throughout some people's lives. Bergamot, lavender and lemongrass make an effective treatment, used regularly in a toner or moisturiser as outlined above.

Cedarwood, juniper and petitgrain are three others to consider and try, as are clary sage and lemon with lavender. There are so many possible causes of spots, and therefore so many possible ways of trying to beat them, that you can only use your common sense and the knowledge contained in my lists of recommended herbs to experiment.

If spots plague the young, wrinkles plague the not so young. These are the oils to try: chamomile, clary sage, fennel, frankincense, geranium, lavender, lemon, neroli, palmarosa, patchouli, rosemary. Use singly or in combinations of two or three. Put five drops of your mixture in the bath. Make up a face-massage treatment with sweet almond oil, two drops of that to one of your essential mixture.

If you just want a really enjoyable bath, and you don't have any special worries about dry skin, spots or anything else, try a mix of two drops each of any three of these: frankincense, geranium, lavender, palmarosa, patchouli, sandalwood, ylang ylang.

Pregnant women

Before using **any** essential oil during pregnancy, check on its safety in the recommended lists of essential oils (see pages 32-68). **Avoid** the following oils completely during the first five months, and only use with great care later with expert advice: clary sage, fennel*, juniper, marjoram, lemon balm, melissa, lemongrass, rosemary.

Avoid ALL OILS not included in the lists unless you have expert advice. Always use smaller quantities – say half the normal amount, of essential oils – unless you do have expert advice.

---

* **Fennel can be useful during pregnancy (*see* P.75) but the stated dosage must not be exceeded.**

These are generally the most useful oils in pregnancy: chamomile, geranium, grapefruit, lavender, sandalwood, tangerine, ylang ylang. For the benefit of those intending to retrieve a silver spoon from the newborn baby's mouth, we could also mention rose and jasmine again.

Pregnant women get tired, they ache, their limbs swell up, they get greasy skin and lifeless hair – all these things are considered normal, or natural. Just because such unpleasantness and exaggerated wear and tear are expected, it doesn't mean you have to suffer it all.

Use natural methods to ease these problems. For example:

Back ache massage: chamomile, geranium and lavender, 3 drops each in 30 ml/2 tbsps carrier oil.

Morning sickness: 1 drop of ginger on the pillow or in bowl of hot water; inhale the steam.

Stretch mark prevention: lavender and tangerine, 5 drops each, in almond and wheatgerm, 30 ml/ 2 tbsps each. Alternatively, use frankincense and tangerine, 3 drops each in 50 ml/3½ tbsps almond or wheatgerm, or both.

Breasts and sore nipples: use the same blends as given above for stretch marks.

Constipation massage: 5 drops patchouli in 20 ml/1¼ tbsps carrier. Alternatively, use 2 drops each of black pepper and fennel in 50 ml/ 3½ tbsps carrier.

Varicose vein prevention: geranium 5 drops, cypress 1 drop, 20 ml/1¼ tbsps carrier; and/or use a couple of drops each of these essential oils in the bath.

Anti-wind massage: fennel, 1 drop per 10 ml/ ¾ tbsp of carrier.

Nausea: lavender 3 drops, fennel 1 drop, mix with honey ad lib, say a couple of tablespoonsfuls. Put a teaspoon of this with a cup of hot water; add a squirt of lemon juice if you like.

Alternatively, gently massage the tummy with fennel, lavender and sandalwood, 2 drops each in 50 ml/3½ tbsps carrier.

Cramp in the legs: cypress and geranium, 2 or 3 drops of each, plus 4 of lavender, added to the bath water.

Tired legs: 2 drops tangerine, 2 drops lavender in 30 ml/2 tbsps carrier.

For tiredness: Revive with lavender and grapefruit, equal amounts. Put half a dozen drops of the mix in the bath, or likewise in 20 ml/1¼ tbsps of carrier oil for a massage.

Sleep with chamomile and lavender in a bedroom burner, or sandalwood, or tangerine and ylang

ylang. Sleep also after a massage with lavender and vetivert, two drops each in 30 ml/2 tbsps carrier.

Fluid retention: massage with cypress, geranium, lavender, two drops each in 30 ml/2 tbsps carrier.

Gentle relaxing massage: chamomile and lavender or sandalwood and ylang yang, 3 drops each to 30 ml/2 tbsps carrier.

Babies

Massaging baby can sometimes be a bit like massaging an eel, but it is good fun for parent and baby alike.

Like any young animal, a human baby cannot get enough cuddling, stroking or petting, and aromatherapy massage is an extremely good form of this because it serves several purposes at once. It helps with the digestive problems, it seems to promote all-round health and contentment, and it's a big ration of cuddles to help the bonding process between parent and child.

Of course with small children it is vital to use only very small amounts of essential oils, and great care must be taken to ensure that you use the right oils. Never experiment on a baby's sensitive skin. In fact, up to three months, **do not use any essential oil other than chamomile and lavender.**

These are helpful oils for upset tummy, or colic. They should be made up into a mixture with 2 drops of each and 40 ml/3¾ tbsps of carrier oil, preferably sweet almond, and massaged ultra-gently into the tummy. Massaging with the blend on chest and back can also promote general well-being and happiness. After three months, more specific blends and oils can be applied. For example:

Colic: chamomile and sweet marjoram, one drop each in 30 ml/2 tbsps carrier, or chamomile and tangerine.

General health: help keep sickness at bay by using essential oils to create a pleasant atmosphere in your baby's room. As well as chamomile, lavender and sandalwood, try eucalyptus or geranium in your daytime burner. Make up a massage mix with 20 ml/1¼ tbsps sweet almond oil plus one drop each of eucalyptus, lavender and tea tree.

Teething: gently rub over the gums a mixture made from a couple of drops of chamomile in half a cup of warm water. Do this several times a day, for a mild, effective method of relief.

Sleeping: promote the right atmosphere for sound sleep with a burner and a few drops each of chamomile and geranium. Another good way is to put a bowl of hot water somewhere nearby, with a few drops of oil added to it.

Young Children

Quite where your offspring stops being a baby and starts being a child is a moot point. In any case, it will be unique in history if it doesn't at some time suffer from cuts, bruises, burns, coughs, hiccups, tummy ache, insect bites, nameless fears and anxieties, over-excitement, and spots. All of these minor yet distressing eventualities can be relieved by using aromatic oils.

Wounds: be prepared, and as your child gets older and more active, add lemon and niaouli to your first-aid kit, which already has eucalyptus, lavender and tea tree. Use these for cleaning and soothing knocks and bashes, scratches and nicks.

Water plus tea tree is a fine antiseptic solution.

Wheatgerm oil plus lavender is an excellent healer for grazed skin.

For burns: use oils you already have – chamomile, eucalyptus, geranium, lavender.A couple of drops of neat lavender on an ice-cold damp flannel, will usually stop a burn from blistering.

For bruises: use a cold compress with geranium and lavender.

For tummy ache: try peppermint or rosemary alone in the massage carrier oil, or with a few drops of chamomile too.

Toothache: oil of cloves is the traditional remedy. Use neat on a cotton bud.

Stings: neat lavender.

Hiccups: massage with fennel, 1 drop to 10 ml/ 1 tbsp of carrier.

Sore skin: chafed skin in winter, for instance, can be relieved with benzoin or myrrh.

In cases of **anxiety and sleeplessness**, a good blend includes chamomile, palmarosa and tangerine, equal amounts. A few drops of this in the bath should help relax.

Try massage also: ten drops of the blend to 30 ml/ 2 tbsps carrier oil, and/or a few drops in a burner at night. Also good in the burner is a blend of benzoin and chamomile. Other oils you can add to your childhood kit, and which are safe for experiments in blends for night-time burning, are frankincense, patchouli and vetivert.

Sporty Types

Four areas of interest here: warming up, cooling down, being exhausted, and being injured.

The best **warming** oils, which should be mixed with a carrier, 3 drops to 50 ml/3¼ tbsps, are benzoin, black pepper, clary sage and ginger. Try them solo or in blends until you find the right mixture for you, and rub them well in at least a quarter of an hour before your workout.

After your **post-exercise** shower, massage in a blend containing two or three oils from this list: benzoin, chamomile, frankincense, lavender, sandalwood and vetivert.

If you think you might get **cramp**, you might be able to prevent it by massage with juniper, lemongrass and marjoram, 3 drops each in 50 ml/3¼ tbsps carrier oil.

For over-exercised bodies there is nothing like a bath, especially if you add to it 3 drops each of lemon and sweet marjoram.

After the bath, a massage is prescribed, using eucalyptus, ginger and peppermint, equal quantities, say 3 drops each in 50 ml/3¼ tbsps carrier oil.

Minor injuries can be eased with baths, massage and compresses using a good blend of oils from a range which should include juniper, sweet marjoram and rosemary.

Those under anxiety and stress

Nothing will stop your body and mind eventually telling you when it's time to stop. If you ignore the warnings there will be a rebellion, an internal coup, and you will regret it. Meanwhile you have obligations, priorities, things to do. There are, as the poet Robert Frost put it, promises to keep, and miles to go before you sleep, and you might well need a bit of help to get you there.

To give you a hand when you need to stand the pace, try a blend of three or four of these: cypress, eucalyptus, geranium, grapefruit, juniper, lavender, peppermint, rosemary.

Add a few drops of your blend to the bath. Even better, get someone to massage you with three drops of it in 30 ml/2 tbsps of carrier. Make up a portable 'sniffer' with a few drops of the neat blend on some cotton wool, and next time you start to drop behind the field, relax for a moment and inhale deeply.

Should you feel in need of a **strengthener** before a stressful event, basil, bergamot and grapefruit make a good blend, perhaps with added lavender if you wish. Chamomile, geranium, lavender and tangerine make a milder blend of the same sort.

If your lack of vitality is more emotional than physical, and you need **spiritual uplift** only, you cannot beat melissa.

The elderly

Apart from serious medical conditions, the worries of elderly people about themselves tend to concern aches and pains, stiffness, and a general feeling that there's a lack of lubrication in the system and the blood doesn't seem to circulate as it once used to.

These are the oils which can help: cypress, geranium, fennel, juniper, lavender. There are others, and these are dealt with under their own headings and under specific treatments for aches and pains and so on, but with what you might call the five oils for the elderly you can provide a good answer to the usual general problems.

Geranium is a good oil for the circulation. It is also an uplifting oil, so it can make you feel more chirpy as well as more confident that the blood is reaching those extremities it had seemingly forgotten about.

Singly or in blends, cypress, juniper and lavender can be used as often as you want, in massages or baths, and fennel is safe too, except for epileptics, provided that excessive quantities are not used, so follow the guidelines given below

A good, general purpose blend for getting the engine turning over smoothly is 3 drops each of cypress, juniper and lavender, plus 5 drops of fennel, in 100 ml/7 tbsps of carrier oil.

Try varying the proportions, within reason, until you find the blend that suits you best.

The terminally ill

Advances in orthodox medicine are enabling terminally ill patients to have better quality of remaining life and alongside that, some doctors and nurses are beginning to show interest in complimentary treatments which they and their colleagues might have dismissed a few years ago.

Often, it is desperation which drives people further and further to the outer fringes of medicine. But not so in this case. Aromatherapy is effective and acceptable, and rapidly expanding in use among the medical professionals.

Terminal illness demands support for its sufferer, which will include physical, psychological and spiritual elements.

The new drugs and delivery systems can control the pain and arrest the disease to some extent, but nowadays the medical team tends to look around more at the other needs, trying to see how that particular patient's personality and circumstances are combining to give what result, and how that can best be treated.

This is the 'holistic' approach, and aromatherapy is part of that. Among the most enthusiastic aromatherapists are those nurses like the Macmillans, dedicated to care of the dying. In terminal disease, the illness is not the only factor to consider. There will be money problems, personal strains, social difficulties, which cannot be treated with drugs and which get worse as the disease progresses. Here the aromatherapist can be knowledgeable, sympathetic, and truly useful.

A few drops of lavender, patchouli and sandalwood mixed with sweet almond, massaged over a good half hour to the accompaniment of soporific music, can provide a brief, blissful remission from the world, relax the patient and enhance the quality of his or her day-to-day existence.

AROMAS ANCIENT AND MODERN

Essential oils help people to look good and feel good, and always have, and so their historical reputation has followed the changing priorities and practices of two great industries: the cosmetic, and the medical. Such matters were, for most of history, closely intertwined. What was considered effective in a perfume, deodorant or skin cream often came from the same plant which supplied treatments for the sick and wounded.

In medicine and therapy, there was a decline in the acceptance of essential oils which lasted for about a hundred years, but aromatherapy, as it has become known this century, has now made a big recovery and is going from strength to strength. But first, the history of aroma cosmetics.

It all starts, like most things, with the ancient civilisations and especially with the Egyptians. By BC 3500, essential oils had probably been well known for the previous 3500 years, to the ancient Chinese and many other civilisations, but this is the time when Egyptian records regularly begin to show that oils were being manufactured, traded and buried with the dead kings and queens.

It was the priests who made the oils and who set the rules about their application, and naturally they kept their lucrative and prestigious trade as secret and mysterious as they could. Secrecy and magic were fine in those days, but the esoteric image still attached to the use of oils is a disadvantage now.

The priests of ancient Egypt mainly used oils made from herbs – spikenard, and members of the oregano family – also citrus fruit, and gums from trees such as myrrh, frankincense, cedar and styrax.

They generally used sesame and almond oils as the carriers.

Spikenard, by the way, is a member of the valerian family (*see* herbs for inducing sleep) and is said to have been the active constituent in the ointment Mary used to anoint the feet of Jesus before the Last Supper.

With its attendant pleasures and rituals, including the application of oils for care of the skin and the increased beauty thereof, bathing has been part of civilisation since it was developed by the Egyptians and the Indians.

Bathing and perfume rituals were taken up in Greece and developed further, and although the Romans were not so interested at first, by the time Nero came to the throne in AD 54, they were total converts and were busy blending oils from flowers, herbs and tree-gums for their stymmata (perfumed ointments).

When the seat of learning moved east from Rome to Constantinople, the perfumed arts became popular with the middle-eastern people who could afford them. The ingredients mostly came from there and to the East.

Although sanitation in medieval and renaissance Europe was notoriously poor, folk were constantly trying all sorts of creams, powders and dyes to improve what nature had left short of the mark. However, while vogues for white lead, butter, pumice powder and baths in wine came and went

(Mary Queen of Scots liked wine baths), the bedrock of the cosmetics industry remained essential oils.

Queen Elizabeth I famously had one bath a year, 'whether she needed it or no', and doubtless was a heavy user of floral aromas to get over the consequences of this. And so it was for a long, long time, the only difference being that the cost of exotic eastern gums and spices led European people to wonder if native plants, such as rosemary and lavender, might not be just as good. Research and practical application proved this to be the case.

In 19th-century France, where cosmetic aromas and therapeutic aromas had already become clearly separated as subjects, they began to apply scientific principles to perfumery. Some of the classic blends of essential oils, using perhaps 20 different ones, began to emerge.

Today they are still important ingredients of all the perfumes you buy, even though many of the constituents of essential oils can now be synthesised. The thing is, no matter how brilliant the chemist, essential oils are so complex that there is always something missing from the artificial equivalent, and therefore they have to add a bit of the real thing to give the perfume its full dimensions. In fact, to a considerable extent, the cost of a perfume is governed by how much of the most expensive essential oils they put in.

No commercial perfume is made from flowers, gums and leaves only. If the scent is to linger long enough and have a sufficient staying-power for the all-day office worker and the all-night reveller, it must also contain animal ingredients, a fact which makes them unacceptable to many people today. These include such substances as musk and castor, (made respectively from the foreskins of deer and beaver), ambergris (intestinal 'stones' excreted by sperm whales), and civet (glandular secretion of civet cats).

The perfume of an essential oil was always its most obvious quality, and sometimes such perfumes became associated with serious matters of the mind and body as well as the more frivolous.

Although the ancients had no electron-beam microscopes, nor could they perform a spectral analysis on oil of juniper, for instance, they could still use it to purify temples and fumigate sick-rooms, and they could see that it did have an effect. They could see that certain oils seemed to be able to put people in certain moods. Priests would use them in incense recipes, knowing that the congregation could thus be helped towards a suitably religious frame of mind.

Above all, people did not know of the existence of micro-organisms. When someone fell sick they had no idea if it was caused by bacterium, fungus or virus, nor did they have any real notion of how the body worked in scientific terms.They did know that you had to eat, and that eating certain things had certain effects, and that some of the illnesses and accidents of life could be treated from the inside and the outside, provided you knew what you were doing with the only medicine available: plants.

Of course, many of their aromatherapy applications were ineffective against the severity of the conditions they hoped to cure. Cancer of the liver, leprosy and gangrene will not respond to herbal potions. But it was all they had, until the last, say, 150 years, and even if there was an understandable desire to protect their professional knowledge with an aura of fear, the witches and the herbal doctors at least had one advantage over medical scientists. They understood that the heart and the mind are part of the same organism.

They knew that the flesh and the spirit could not be treated as if they were totally separate, as if a therapist were a mechanic working on either the electrics or the rear suspension. However, as conventional medicine became widely accepted, things which could not be seen under a microscope were deemed not to exist and everything other than science became 'alternative'.

Now, there is a chink of light showing where the firmly closed door of medical science has been cautiously unlocked. All but the most obstinate are admitting that the herbal tradition has something to offer, and maybe there is something in these oils, and possibly those old doctors from Babylon, Thebes and Athens did know a thing or two.

Elsewhere in the world, in India and China for example, the herbal tradition has never been broken. Doctors are practising much the same treatments and therapies as they were 2000 years ago, but in the West, which has a different definition of civilisation, the only voices recently raised for herbs and their oils were those of a very few isolated individuals.

The term 'aromatherapy' was coined by a French chemist called René-Maurice Gattefossé who worked for the family perfume company. One day – according to the story it was in 1928 – he burned his finger and thrust the painful part into the nearest pot of cool liquid – which happened to be one of his perfume ingredients, oil of lavender.

He noticed that the burn healed up faster than normal and left no scar, which benefits he attributed to the lavender oil.

Any medieval apothecary could have told him this, and any ancient Egyptian priest could have told him that a mixture of cedarwood and myrrh would do the same job, but such knowledge had been forgotten and M. Gattefossé had yet to rediscover it. The results of his experiments appeared in his book Aromathérapie, published in 1937.

For the next 50 years, aromatherapy remained almost unknown, and a cause for ridicule to those who were familiar with the term. Nevertheless, another 20 years have seen the widespread acceptance of the practice throughout the western world, with millions of people accepting that essential oils have therapeutic qualities which can benefit them in many spheres of their life.

GLOSSARY

Absolute a pure and concentrated form of essential oil, often very viscous (*see* below) and sometimes solid. It is prepared by dissolving the wanted elements – the oil – from the concrete (*see* below) using pure alcohol, leaving the unwanted waxes and impurities behind.

Concrete the product of an extraction process used when distillation (*see* below) is not possible, usually because heat affects the qualities of the oil. The plant material is put through chemical solvents and the resulting soup is called a concrete, tending to be stronger and longer lasting than the usual essential oil.

Distillation the method by which most oils are extracted from their parent plants. The plants are boiled in water or have steam driven through. The steam, now carrying dissolved substances from the plant, is taken off and cooled rapidly. The resulting liquor has essential oil in it which will float to the surface, leaving a highly perfumed flower water.

Effleurage the masseur's term for stroking.

Expression a method of oil production by pressing (sometimes by hand), for instance ripe orange peel.

Notes top notes, middle notes, base notes. These are not, as you might think, to do with the artful mixing of aroma cocktails but are a scientific classification of oils.

The speed at which they evaporate – their volatility – is put for convenience into three broad bands. Rapidly evaporating – highly volatile – oils are called top notes, slowly evaporating oils are base notes.

Volatility seems to coincide quite well with broad categories of essential-oil properties. Generally, top notes are the more invigorating types, and base notes the more soothing.

When making a blend, you add the top notes last and expect them to be the first to make an impact. As they evaporate, they leave the middle and the base notes behind.

Olfactory of or pertaining to the sense of smell.

Petrissage masseur's name for squeezing/kneading.

Tapotement masseur's tapping or patting.

Viscosity if it's viscous, it's thick and sticky, and some oils have higher viscosity than others. For example, benzoin and sandalwood are more viscous, but this is perfectly natural and does not mean the oil has deteriorated.

INDEX

INDEX OF OILS

As the flower of roses in the spring of the year, as lilies by the rivers of waters, and as the branches of the frankincense tree in the time of summer.

ECCLESIASTICUS 50